What Responsibilities Does a Jewish Person Have in Rel...

What Are Jewish Families Like?

Did God Need the Rest...

Is It Hard F...

...Commemorate?

...the Hardest Part of Being a Bar/Bat Mitzvah?

What Does Israel Represent to Y...

...d Create the Day for Another Reason?

What Is Your Favorite Part of How Passover I...

"As I Learn about the Bible, It Teaches Me That God..."

...ead the Jewish People Out of Egypt?

What Miracle in Jewish History Is the Most Extraordinary?

...Other Jews and Judaism?

Are There Any Special Ways That Your Family Celebrates Shabbat?

What Have You Learned from Your Parents (or Grandparents) about Being Jewish?

Why Did God Select Moses to Lead...

How Is the Jewish Religion Similar or Different from Other Religions?

Why Is Chanukah Called 'The Festival of Lights'?

We Gave the World Moses and Bagels

The Jewish Publication Society gratefully acknowledges
the generous gift made in support of this book:

לדור ודור

Lovingly dedicated to our parents,
children, and grandchildren
In appreciation of Jewish continuity

Norma Levy Shapiro and Bernard Shapiro

We Gave the World
Moses
and
Bagels

Art and Wisdom
of Jewish Children

David Heller, Ph.D.

THE JEWISH PUBLICATION SOCIETY
PHILADELPHIA
2000 • 5760

The Jewish Publication Society
2100 Arch Street, 2nd Floor
Philadelphia, PA 19103-1399

Design by Susan Deikman

Cover illustrations:
  Valerie Levin (front)
  Lauren Kutner (back)

Manufactured in China

09 08 07 06 05 04 03 02 01 00   10 9 8 7 6 5 4 3 2 1

Library of Congress Cataloging-in-Publication Data

We gave the world Moses and bagels: art and wisdom of Jewish children/[edited by]
David Heller.--1 st ed.

    p. cm.
    ISBN 0-8276-0688-5

    1. Jewish way of life--Quotations, maxims, etc. 2. Jewish children--United
    States--Quotations. 3. Children's drawings--United States. I. Heller, David.

    BM727.W4 2000
    96'.083--dc21   99-05271 (

With love for my wife, Elizabeth;
in honor of my parents,
Mark and Blanche Heller;
and in memory of my grandparents,
the Hellers and the Goldmans

A Note From the Publisher

When we invited young artists between the ages of five and ten to participate in a nation-wide art contest, we never dreamed that so many children would respond so enthusiastically. To our delight,

more than twelve hundred boys and girls from the United States and Canada submitted their work for review. By the time we stopped counting, our office was filled with boxes and boxes of children's art!

As the art was sorted by age-level and category in the weeks that followed, we found ourselves touched by the children's insights, their passion for their Jewish heritage. And each afternoon, as staff members circled the conference room table to look at the many drawings— of *dreidels*, Noah's arks, Towers of Babel, kiddush cups, and more—you could hear their laughter and ooh's and ahh's echoing down the hall.

Once the JPS staff chose the semifinalists, Danielle Rice, Curator of Education, and Marla K. Shoemaker, Assistant Curator at the Philadelphia Museum of Art, were kind enough to help us narrow down the semifinalists to the artists whose work appears in these pages. Each brought to the review process a professional educator's eye, a love of children, and, of course, a keen sense of color and design, all of which are reflected in the winning art work.

To all of the children who were kind enough to enter the contest and to all of the parents and teachers who helped them, JPS would like to express its deepest appreciation. Their enthusiasm and passion for being Jewish—and their creativity in expressing their Judaism—served as an inspiration to us all. And we hope their art, combined with the children's responses to David Heller's questions, will serve as an inspiration to readers of all faiths and ages.

Arielle, age 9

Introduction

If being Jewish is simply a way to celebrate life, then children are among our leading celebrants. Brimming with lessons learned in Hebrew school, in synagogue, or in temple, or at home with mother and father, Jewish children offer a lively and colorful account of what it means to be Jewish. Their original interpretations of modern Jewish life are frequently as educational as they are heartwarming. The children's vibrancy, as expressed through their views of mitzvot and matzah alike, is a joy to behold—and it is the purpose of this collection to bring their notions of Judaism to life.

In describing what it means to be Jewish, Abraham Heschel said that the Jewish people "are the track of God in the wilderness." That is quite a legacy to uphold, but the youngsters in this collection, ages four to twelve, are placing their own little footprints down as they describe their own uniquely Jewish journeys. These children were contacted through schools and synagogues or temples, and all agreed to be interviewed for approximately one hour concerning the meaning of being a Jew. I am indebted to my small consultants for their time and effort, and I find myself in awe of their creativity and wisdom—qualities which seem unmistakenly heaven-sent in the children. It is my privilege to share their observations and commentaries about Jewish life with you.

What do the youngsters comment upon? Everything under the sun. They freely associate to what it means to be Jewish and what Jewish families have in common. They discuss the Bible and the biblical figures who are among their early heroes and heroines: Abraham, Jacob, Moses, Miriam, and Esther, among others. With glee, they depict their holiday

experiences, and they revel in telling about Jewish customs, rituals, and that highest aspect of Jewish life—Jewish food! But amidst these cultural interests, the youngsters also reveal their spiritual beliefs as well, as they speak of God with great reverence, with familiarity, and with love.

In the pages that follow, Jewish children from all levels of observance share their personal beliefs. It is my hope that you will find the children's ideas a joy to behold and feel, as I do, that the children have much to teach us about what it means to be Jewish.

—David Heller, Ph.D.

Adina, age 10

"To Be Jewish Means..."

"It's like riding in a blue and white balloon...and it's up to God to say where the balloon should go." —**Judy, age 12**

"Watching the movie *The Ten Commandments* every year at Passover." —**Beth H., age 9**

"Saying the *ha-Motzi* when you are supposed to." —**Amy T., age 8**

"It's being a mensch seven days a week." —**Brian, age 10**

"Studying the Torah." —**Carey, age 10**

"Believing in one God and not believing in idols that have no clothes on." —**Marna, age 9**

"Helping others whenever you can. It's that simple."
—Esther, age 11

"Celebrating Shabbat and thinking about Shabbat on Monday and Tuesday, not just Friday night."
—Ariel, age 7

"Going to synagogue, following the 613 Commandments, and being nice to your sister—even if the last thing is hard to do."
—Allan, age 10

"Being true to God and to your faith, even if it makes you feel different sometimes."
—Gabriel, age 10

"Being a part of a religious people that sure seems to like sponge cake a lot."
—Alex, age 9

"Praying to God day and night and even in-between meals."
—Mitchell, age 11

"Remembering to do the *Shema* and realizing it's just as important as washing your face or brushing your teeth in the morning."
—Joel, age 9

Valerie, age 8

"Believing that having chicken soup is better than eating a steak."
—Marty K., age 11

"Never feeling like a stranger to other Jewish people."
—Judah, age 5

"To trust in the Lord and do it with your whole heart and mind."
—Kenneth, age 12

Adina, age 6

What Do Most Jewish People Have in Common?

"We know how to say the 'ch' sound without giving ourselves laryngitis." —**Elise, age 11**

"We eat knishes." —**Sharon, age 6**

"We get circumcised...Well, at least the boys do and then they make a big fuss and throw the little kid a party after he stops complaining." —**Alex, age 11**

"We are all trying to set the world's record for good deeds in one lifetime." —**Mallory, age 11**

"We are against oppression and prejudice whenever it happens... And plus we're big on having a conscience." —**Ed B., age 9**

"A lot of us have dark hair but my mom actually doesn't... I wonder how she got her hair changed?" —**Lillie, age 6**

"We go to services on Saturdays but then we have all day on Sunday to watch football." —Richard, age 9

"I think Jewish people all worry a lot...It probably comes from all the trouble they've had over the years with bad people." —Jacob, age 10

"Most Jewish people once came from places like Russia and Poland...Now they mostly come from places like California and New Jersey or anywhere else they can put a synagogue." —Justin, age 9

"I think most Jewish people miss their mother a lot when they don't see her." —Aliya, age 6

"We all celebrate Shabbat...I've been doing it for a long time now." —Erica, age 6

"Sometimes, we all think about the Holocaust and it brings tears to our eyes." —Alana, age 9

שלום

"The Torah is kind of like a member of our family... We can't live happy lives without it." —**Ryan, age 11**

"We believe in God, we study the laws, and deep down, we believe that everything in life does work out for the best once we get to Heaven and see what God has in store for us." —**Rose, age 11**

"Most of us know how to make an *alef*, but all of us know how to have God in our hearts." —**Vlade, age 9**

Shira, age 11

"The Thing I Like Best about Being Jewish Is..."

"Drinking more grape juice at religious events than just about any other religion in the world." —**Marissa, age 7**

"Even when you have to start school in September, you can cheer up because you know you are going to have a few holidays coming up real soon." —**Steven, age 9**

"How people look up to you when you do a mitzvah." —**David B., age 7**

"Reciting prayers and feeling good about myself because of it." —**Carey, age 10**

"Eating bagels and cream cheese and feeling like it's part of my heritage." —**Avram, age 11**

"Being unique...I might be the only kid in my public school class who has Moses as an ancestor." —**Josh, age 11**

“Singing songs together that have been sung for a thousand years... 'Aitz Chaim' is one of them.**”**
—**Perry, age 12**

“Talking to God....
But eating raisin challah is in second place.**”**
—**Sheryl, age 8**

“The caring...Judaism is good at teaching you to value that, and that's something that a kid can admire.**”**   —**Larry, age 8**

“My parents are the best thing about being Jewish...They kinda went with the religion. It was a package deal and it's worked out really good for my brother and me.**”**
—**Robert J., age 10**

Sofia, age 10

What Are the Three Most important Things for a Jewish Person to Have?

"A loving family, *mezuzzahs* in your house, and then maybe it's good to have a watch with Hebrew letters on it.**"**
—**Robert, age 10**

"Three grandchildren...That's why my grandma says she is the happiest person you will ever meet.**"**
—**Afton, age 8**

"A prayer book, a big Bible that's easy to read, and then a cat...I don't know why a cat is important, but I just think it would be nice to add to the family.**"**
—**Aliya, age 6**

"A challah, a backup challah, and a third challah...You can never have too much challah.**"**
—**Dale, age 8**

"You need a loving mother, a loving father, and then you need God—most of the other stuff in life is in second place to those three.**"**
—**Zlotka, age 10**

What Have You Learned from Your Parents (or Grandparents) about Being Jewish?

"That being Jewish kinda sticks with you like it was glued inside your sweater."
—**Jayne, age 9**

"Your parents teach you how to say *'Baruch'* when you are pretty small."
—**Aliya, age 6**

"My grandparents taught me the meaning of a few Yiddish words and a lot of English ones, such as 'charity.'"
—**David B., age 7**

"My father taught me to be kind to animals and not treat my dog like a slave, since we were once slaves in Egypt and we don't like that much either."
—**Larry, age 8**

"I think a lot of Jewish parents are like mine: they teach you about prayers and the importance of Jewish history."
—**Carey, age 10**

Igor, age 8

"They all taught me how to light a match...That's important because Jewish people are always lighting candles."
—Brittany, age 12

"That being Jewish is a good way to eat good food and learn about God too."
—Jessica, age 8

"My parents taught me that being Jewish is a blessing."
—Howard, age 10

"My grandpa taught me to smile when I say 'good yuntif.'"
—Eddie, age 8

"My family taught me that we are related to the Christian peoples, and that we shouldn't let misunderstandings get in the way of friendship."
—Donna, age 11

"I think the biggest thing I've learned is that families are the best place to learn about love."
—Mindy, age 9

Lauren, age 9

What Are Jewish Families Like?

❝They're like everybody else except for Moses is more of a hero to them than Michael Jordan is.❞
—**Robert, age 10**

❝Some of them speak Yiddish so well you would think God taught it right to them.❞
—**Ed B., age 9**

❝All Jewish families have pretty *mezuzzahs* on their doors.❞
—**Aliya, age 6**

❝They hug you a lot and kiss you on the cheek...If you don't mind that, you will probably get along with them real well.❞
—**Toby, age 9**

"They're warm and friendly and they don't mind piling in and having a big slumber party in your living room." —Andi, age 10

"Some families touch lights on Shabbat but a lot of people don't... The main thing the families try to teach children is to be kind to others." —Carey, age 10

"They worry a lot about sicknesses...Like if you have a cold, they drown you in soup and act like you have pneumonia." —Shari, age 9

"Some of them are like the families in Fiddler on the Roof... Except they don't sing so much and the modern men do more shaving." —Aaron, age 9

Cara, age 7

❝ Well, if you go by the Tower of Babel story, God isn't real into architecture. ❞
—Rob, age 11

❝ The way I see God is that God could be a He or a She, but for sure God is making everything all better for us. ❞
—Ben, age 9

“Never misses a Rosh Hashanah service.**”** —**Simon, age 4**

“Created the whole world and that's how we started breathing and saying 'Shalom' to each other.**”** —**Irvin, age 8**

“Loves girls the same as boys...But I have to admit He was pretty bummed out and disappointed about that Eve lady.**”** —**Irene, age 9**

“God does believe in punishment so people can learn...But it makes Him sad and He only does that when He has to, like the golden calf scene.**”** —**Mark P., age 8**

“God helps people to get across the deserts that they run into in their lives.**”** —**Shira, age 12**

“Made everybody in His image...even my brother.**”** —**Bill, age 11**

Avital, age 6

"I think God is like a candy store that is always filled with love." —**Shoshana, age 6**

"He's in a lot of good stories, like Jonah and the whale, and God is the one who usually saves somebody or gives them another chance when He can." —**Allan, age 10**

"He's sort of like the earth and the water... God is everywhere." —**Bettie, age 9**

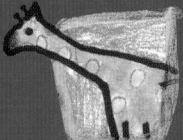

"God is everywhere you go....Even near the principal's office at school." —**Larry, age 8**

"God is kind to animals...That's why God lined them up right on time to go sailing on Noah's Ark."
—Steven, age 7

Kate, age 7

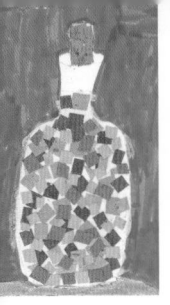

Did God Need the Rest on the Seventh Day o

"God already had a headache from hearing Adam and Eve argue over who was going to clean the Garden...He needed some peace and quiet.**"**
—Gary, age 11

"God never gets tired. He's not like a person. But He just wanted to look around at all the birds and the other stuff and see that it was made pretty good.**"**
—Aliya, age 6

"Making light was what got God exhausted...Later on, God let Thomas Edison do the work for Him.**"**
—Eli, age 10

"God figured that if He could convince people to rest and stay out of mischief, then He could find more time to pray and listen to their prayers.**"**
—Hilary, age 9

"The day of rest is a spiritual day...Our bodies rest while our minds are busy working their way toward God.**"** —Janet, age 11

Did God Create the Day for Another Reason?

"He rested from all the worrying He was doing. He was worried that some of the animals would come out speaking English or some of the fish would fly, but everything turned out just right." —Rivka, age 8

"Sure He needed the rest. If you just did an operation on a man's rib and made a girl out of it, you would need a rest too." —Ryan, age 11

"God didn't need rest but God noticed a bunch of angels huffin' and puffin' and so God said: 'Okay, okay, let's take five. Report to work on Sunday at 10 A.M. sharp!'" —Frieda, age 9

"God just wanted to create a special day so that we would remember the blessing of creation for all time." —Carey, age 10

Arielle, age 9

Are There Any Special Ways That Your Family Celebrates Shabbat?

"We say our prayers on the candles, and we never forget to drink the grape juice."
—**Carey, age 10**

"It's the only time in the whole week when the family isn't rushing around and frantic, and even the kids don't mind."
—**Marty K., age 11**

"It's the one day when it really feels like God is sitting at our dinner table."
—**Ellen B., age 11**

"We invite Christian people over and we talk about our ideas about God and then we have dessert together."
—**Charna, age 9**

"We shut off the lights in the whole house and we put on candles...It's not spooky; it's actually a lot of fun."
—**Carole, age 7**

Noah, age 8

"We eat challah as fast as the challah bakers can make it." —Eddie, age 8

"We go to synagogue and sometimes my father gets an *aliyah*...He's usually number five in the batting order." —**Todd, age 11**

"We see our friends in *shul* and we find out how they survived another week in school too." —**Alex, age 9**

"For us, it's something like Thanksgiving every week. It's not just that we eat turkey and rice a lot, it's that we take time out to thank God for all that we have." —**Alan, age 11**

"Shabbat is a day of rest...I'm good at resting because mostly I've been practicing all week." —**Steven, age 7**

"The thing I have noticed about my family is that we just seem to smile a lot more on Shabbat than we do on Mondays or Tuesdays...Maybe we feel a little closer to God on Shabbat." —**Hannah, age 9**

Adina, age 10

How Does God Communicate with People?

"If I was God, I would write little notes to us on scribble pads."
—Judah, age 5

"God talks in a language that you can understand, but it might take awhile to get to your arms and legs so you can change how you behave."
—Rachel, age 10

"God doesn't use a fax machine or anything like that...He's more on the old-fashioned side."
—Nathan, age 9

"God used to talk out loud...But now he kinda whispers inside of you and you can still hear Him good if you listen real closely."
—Carey, age 10

"God uses floods or other things that might get our attention."
—**Mindy, age 9**

"He blows the shofar to let us know it's time to pray."
—**Simon, age 4**

"God finds some Jewish man or lady and they do something like make the sun stand still, but then they end up saying: 'Hey, I can't take the credit. All the glory belongs to God.'"
—**Jacob, age 10**

"Maybe God has messengers. Somebody named Gabriel was one, and then maybe the mail people do it for Him now."
—**Carol, age 5**

"I think once God talked to Moses through a burning bush. That was cool. But if God wants to talk to me, He doesn't have to go to all that trouble. All He needs to do is answer my prayers."
—**Grant, age 9**

Judah, age 9

The Children's Views on the Forefathers of the Jewish People

"Like it says in the Midrash, Abraham smashed the idols and put the object in the biggest idol's hand to make it look like it was an inside job...That was quick thinking for an ancient guy."
—**Rich, age 12**

"You got to give Abraham credit for always trying to find righteous people...I wonder how hard that would be now."
—**Donna, age 11**

"Isaac had courage...He had to, since he went up to that mountaintop with his father, when his father had that knife in his hands and a funny look on his face."
—**Myron, age 9**

"Jacob was really smart because he knew how to get the best blessing from Isaac...Of course, you could say Jacob was a little shifty."
—**Joel, age 9**

"Jacob was a better wrestler than the ones we have today...
Plus he didn't dress in a costume and act wild all the time.**"**
                                                           —**Larry, age 8**

"Joseph got treated unfairly because of his beautiful coat.
But he ended up okay, and he taught his brothers a few
things about forgiveness.**"**
                                                           —**Jennifer, age 10**

"Joseph is someone I admire. Even though he was sold into
slavery, he had faith in God that things would come to a good
purpose in the end.**"**
                                                           —**Carey, age 10**

"Moses was kind of a forefather, except he spent some time
as an Egyptian so I hope that doesn't disqualify him.**"**
                                                           —**Mirna, age 10**

"Moses reminds me of my grandfather...Only difference is
my grandfather doesn't change rods into snakes or make the
water turn colors, as far as I know.**"**
                                                           —**Johanna, age 7**

What Were Some of the Best Known Biblical Heroines Like? (such as Sarah, Miriam, and Esther)

"Those ladies stood up for their rights and wouldn't take 'No, ma'am' for an an answer."
—Shana, age 8

"None of those girls ever gave up. Sarah didn't give up when she wanted a baby. She had faith and she kept on being a wife until God showed her the way." —Beth B., age 10

"Miriam snuck Moses down the river and then God did the steering.... God depended on a lot of the women to get the ball rolling." —Mindy, age 9

"I think maybe those ladies were a little bit nicer to their brothers than I am to my brother." —Aliya, age 6

"They all wore dresses because Bible ladies didn't wear pants or jeans in those days." —Samantha, age 7

"All were kind and caring, and pretty famous too since they were written up in the Bible, and just think of all the synagogues with Bibles in them." —Carey, age 10

"Girls like Rachel and Leah had a lot of physical strengths because they came from a long line of shepherds, who needed to keep in tip-top shape." —Mallory, age 11

"Many of the Jewish women had great courage...and one other important thing—they all knew how to make bread and matzah." —Amy J., age 9

"All of the Bible women like Sarah had the ability to keep up the family even if their husbands were off preaching somewhere." —Alexis, age 12

eir husbands had to accept that too." —**Allan, age 10**

Sarah, age 7

Why Did God Select Moses to Lead the Jewish People Out of Egypt?

"Moses was a strong person and he wasn't afraid of Pharaoh, except maybe once when he saw Pharaoh's chariot had spikes on it."

—Marshall, age 12

"I heard it was because Moses was related to God's fifth cousin."
—Dean R., age 6

"Moses was a good leader and he could climb mountains good."
—Merrill, age 5

"Moses finally realized that he was Jewish, and he decided to act Jewish, even though he could have taken the easier road and chosen to act like an Egyptian prince."
—Carey, age 10

"Moses did things that people liked...like juggle rocks and tablets."
—Kenny, age 7

"Moses was a person who cared for the people no matter who they were."
—Estelle, age 10

"God really wanted to pick Miriam, Moses' sister. But God knew the people back then were sexist, and besides, Miriam didn't like the desert that much anyway."
—Rose, age 11

Sydney, age 9

"He was tall and strong and he was a good actor when they came across mean border guards in the desert."

—Bonnie, age 8

"Moses had a good sense of direction and that's important when there's only one good way to get to the Promised Land."

—Ellen, age 9

"Moses had a lisp. God thought that if He gave Moses this mission, Moses could finally get over his inferiority complex."

—Marian, age 11

"He was just plain brave and he had a lot of faith...That's the real story behind it."

—Lenore, age 9

What Do You Think the Average Person's First Words Might Have Been When He or She Saw the Ten Commandments?

"These are hard to memorize. I hope they have Cliff Notes for these commandments."
—**Rich, age 12**

"Wow, gee whiz, golly, God wasn't kiddin' about laying down some strict laws for us!"
—**Dana, age 11**

"This comes as quite a surprise...Maybe we should talk to our lawyer about these commandments before we sign anything."
—**Carey, age 10**

"Maybe we could just try to obey the even numbered ones first. That would be easier."
—**Rosalyn, age 10**

"Good rules to follow. But I don't think they'll last too long in places like New York."
—**Danny, age 9**

"The people just said the *Shema* and they looked up in awe."
—**Shira, age 10**

What Is Your Favorite Part of How Passover Is Celebrated?

"Hiding the *afikoman*...It gives me a chance to bargain with my grandpa."

—**Aliya, age 6**

"Eating the meal...I like the gefilte fish the most."

—**Carey, age 10**

"How Passover is eight days of fun instead of just one."

—**Renee, age 9**

"When my mom gets a big smile on her face because she can see everybody is enjoying the chicken she made."

—**Danny, age 9**

"When funny things happen like when this kid I know put a whole spoon of horseradish in his mouth and his face turned red...Surprisingly, he wanted some more later in the seder."

—**Frieda, age 9**

"I like how all the parts of the seder have a special meaning...When else can you sit down at dinner and have a meal that is so meaningful?"

—Joshua, age 10

EGG

CHAROSET

פסח

SALT WATER

PARSLEY

BITTER HERB

SHANK BONE

Alina, age 8

"There's nothing like looking for the middle matzah and finding it three weeks later in the piano."

—Kara, age 9

"Seeing your grandparents is the best...It makes a kid feel special because you realize how seeing you makes their day."

—Art, age 9

"I like how there's four cups of wine spread out across the night, but actually I'm a juice man myself."   —Schaeffer, age 10

"The unleavened bread symbol shows that we are close to our ancestors...It makes me feel a part of Jewish history."

—Lisa C., age 11

"'Had Gadyah' is one of my favorite songs...I wonder if anybody ever put it on a record?"

—Aaron, age 9

"When we open the door for Elijah...I think he must like to come to our house because we put out some Passover cookies for him next to his cup of wine."

—Becky, age 10

What Does Purim Commemorate?

"How Esther was a queen...She was the type who wanted to make pastries and save her people." —Glenn, age 9

"It's all about prejudice and how it hurts people...But in the end, goodness and understanding will win out." —Baruch, age 9

"It has to do with when they hung Haman and how it created a big enough story to make a holiday out of." —Carey, age 10

"When the people didn't have a lot of time, so they ate hamantaschen because you could make them quick." —Lauren, age 7

"Purim is about victory for the Jewish people—plus it's a good reason to have a party with funny hats on." —Edward B., age 9

"Purim is a noisy holiday where you get to block out names...What kid wouldn't like that?" —Johanna, age 7

Why Is Chanukah Called the "Festival of Lights"?

66 Just like the lamps stayed lit for a long time, the Jewish people have lasted for centuries. 99
—Frieda, age 9

66 The Israelites thought they only had enough oil for one day, but God made a miracle and it stretched out for eight. 99
—Carey, age 10

66 The miracle I would really like to see is a *dreidel* spinning for eight days...Now that would be amazing 99
—Steven, age 7

66 They had to call it that so it didn't get called 'The Festival of Presents.' 99
—Ryan, age 11

66 Chanukah is not just about menorah lights; it's about how there's a light in us that burns in an eternal way. 99
—Aviva, age 12

"One good reason would be that all the Jewish kids' faces light up when they see the menorah, and of course, when those eight presents start rolling in."

—Ben, age 9

Ilana, age 10

What Do You Think about Most during Yom Kippur, the Day of Atonement?

"Eating a huge chocolate bar once the fast is over."
—Brittany, age 12

"Turkey and roast beef and chicken...But then I ask for forgiveness, because I realize we had to kill some animals to make all those foods."
—Lenore, age 9

"I think about how I love being Jewish but how my feet are killing me during the last part of the service."
—Alexis, age 12

"I pray for the end of all wars, and I pray for a reduction in homework for all the children of the world."
—Scott P., age 9

"I pray for my family, and the people in the synagogue, and the people and the animals of the world who have no home."
—Laura, age 8

"I just concentrate on God...I think about all the good things God has done for the world."

—Carey, age 10

"All that time I wasted during the year on video games... I ask God to understand, and I hope maybe He has played a few video games too."

—Alex J., age 10

"Some people think about people they know who have died... It's nice that the love keeps on going."

—Eli, age 10

"I think about music, because when I think about music I feel closer to God."

—Alisha, age 12

Amy, age 7

What Miracle in Jewish History Is the Most Extraordinary?

"That we are still alive and kicking after all these thousands of years." —**Wendy M., age 11**

"Crossing the Red Sea...On your average day, you usually can't get a miracle out of raising up a stick." —**Carey, age 10**

"Those lions that decided to have a picnic with Daniel...You would think they could have a feast with Daniel as the main part of the meal!" —**Todd, age 11**

"If I ever make it through my Bar Mitzvah, that would be right up there in the top ten miracles." —**Alex J., age 10**

"The creation of human beings was the greatest miracle... How did God do it without making a lady wait nine months to have a baby?" —**Robert, age 10**

"Making the walls of Jericho come down...I guess it pays to know how to play the trumpet."

—Rich, age 11

"If you count Eve as Jewish, being made out of a rib isn't exactly something you see a lot of."

—Dani, age 8

"Oil lamps that keep on going are miracles; winning the lottery isn't, but some people might be silly enough to believe it is."

—Lisa C., age 11

"My idea of a miracle is when that whale knew the guy had learned his lesson...So the whale just spit the guy out right on cue from God."

—Adam S., age 8

"Samson's strength was kind of a miracle because they didn't have Nautilus equipment or free weights in those days."

—Joshua, age 10

"The spirit and survival of the Jewish people is a miracle, but to tell you the truth, I think God planned it all along."

—Ellen, age 9

Reflections on the Great Kings: What Are King David and King Solomon Known For?

"David was great with a slingshot and Solomon was good with being wise, but that Goliath guy probably wished it was the other way around."
                                                            —Adam C., age 9

"David is known for his star...The other guy should have found a symbol too. It's good for publicity."
                                                            —Stan, age 10

"Solomon was famous for his wisdom. But he took a real chance with telling that baby's mother to divide him up, plus that could have caused the baby to poop while the king was holding him."
                                                            —Lenore, age 9

"They both wrote neat poems and they had careers as writers, but they couldn't take too much of the credit since it was all inspired by God."
                                                            —Bruce, age 10

"One thing for sure: they were both brave in all kinds of Bible ways."
—Carey, age 10

"They were like the early presidents of Israel...Something like Abraham Lincoln, except they weren't so skinny."
—Eddie, age 8

"David played the harp...I think Solomon may have played the harmonica with him."
—Moshe, age 7

"Both of them built up Jerusalem out of gold and silver...But you know, a good architect could have probably saved them a lot of money."
—Jacob, age 10

"Both men were proud of their accomplishments, such as when David slew Goliath, but in the end it was really their love for God that made them stand out."
—Rachel P., age 10

What Jewish Symbol or Ritual Do You Like the Best?

“The Star of David...I like how there are two triangles that cross over each other to make a perfect symbol.”
—Toni, age 10

“Eating challah...It's the best Jewish ritual because it's so fluffy and full of dough.”
—Carey, age 10

“I like the Israeli flag because blue and white are my favorite colors...But you have to make sure not to get it dirty because it has so much white in it.”
—Alissa, age 7

“Saying prayers is really good...It lets you talk to God.”
—Aliya, age 6

Maddie, age 6

"The *etrog* and the *lulav*...They make me feel closer to nature and it's cool to feel like a farmer in the Bible days."
—**Dani, age 8**

"Fire is an important symbol because it was created by God and it's a sign of life, like when you light candles on Friday night...But water is important too, because you have to have it around so the house doesn't burn down!"
—**Brittany, age 12**

"Facing east when I pray...It gives you a sense of direction for your life too."
—**Lea, age 12**

"Not eating pork...I can bet you that this ritual is real popular with the pig population. They probably say to each other in Pig Latin: 'I love Jewish people. They're so humane. That's my favorite human religion.'"
—**Dov, age 10**

"Throwing crumbs into the river to show you are letting go of sins...It's a good way to show God that you are going to improve."
—**Raphael, age 8**

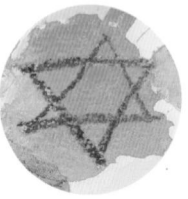

What Jewish Food Do You Consider to Be the Most Delicious?

"Matzah—because it can't go flat on you because it already is flat!" —**Jacob, age 10**

"Passover Cheerios." —**Aliya, age 6**

"Hamantaschen...We have the best food shaped like a hat in the world." —**Moshe, age 7**

"Bagels are probably the most popular Jewish food, but if it's a pizza bagel does it count as Jewish or just plain ol' American?" —**Shari, age 8**

Lauren, age 7

"Charoset...It tastes sweet but it helps if you don't think about how you are supposed to be eating bricks." —**Hannah, age 9**

"Matzah ball soup...It has a special taste. I liked it so much when I was small that I named one of my grandmother's 'Grandma Soup.'" —**Carey, age 10**

"I'm a parsley fan...Passover is one of my big days of the year." —**Aliya, age 6**

"Egg *kechels* are the best. But I was wondering, could they put chocolate chips in them?" —**Dale, age 8**

"There's some fruit we ate on Sukkot that was really different…I think they call it 'pom-poms.'"
—**Meredith, age 8**

"I make my Mom buy halavah. But they should try to moosh it into ice cream and make a new flavor. I bet Ben and Jerry would try it out."
—**Ariel, age 7**

"Latkes are number one…Even though we have to wait all year to eat the really good ones on Chanukah."
—**Andrew M., age 8**

"Grape juice is one of the best Jewish foods, but it's also created the most stains on Jewish rugs…or even Persian ones for that matter."
—**Robin C., age 9**

What is the Most Desirable Aspect of Being a Bar/Bat Mitzvah?

"All of a sudden, you aren't a squirt anymore."

—**Robert, age 10**

"You get to have napkins with your name on them and that makes you feel like a very important person."

—**Mitchell, age 11**

"You can finally say: 'Gee, Hebrew is no sweat. It's like a second language to me.'"

—**Bruce, age 10**

"You might be able to read the Torah and impress your friends who used to think you were just a goofball."

—**Carin, age 11**

"When I get Bar Mitzvahed, I plan on inviting a hundred kids...It will be educational for them and just think of all those presents!"

—**Gamliel, age 8**

"You get to drink Manischewitz wine like a grown-up."

—**Judd, age 9**

"The best part might be seeing the pride your parents feel, but the big cake at the end isn't bad either."

—**Becky, age 10**

"I think the chance to express myself might be very important to me, and it might be for other Bat Mitzvah kids too."

—**Elise, age 11**

"Nothing can beat the good feelings you get for making a charity donation to celebrate your big day."

—**Leonard, age 12**

"It's all good practice for your wedding...I think that on Bar Mitvahs people should throw bagels at you instead of rice!"

—**Melody, age 11**

"The best part of being a Bar Mitvah is you feel like you are really becoming a member of the Jewish people."

—**Raymond, age 12**

What Is the Hardest Part of Being a Bar/Bat Mitzvah?

"Having to wear a tie...In my book, that's asking too much."
—**Alex, age 9**

"Practicing, practicing, practicing."
—**Ryan, age 11**

"Being scared to death that your voice might crack in the middle of the haftorah."
—**Ed B., age 9**

"Sitting through the hour-long sermon when all you can think about is the party afterward."
—**Brittany, age 12**

"Having to wait to have your Bat Mitzvah until after the tax season, because Bat Mitzvahs are so expensive and because your father is an accountant."
—**Mallory, age 11**

"Having to sing a lot in Hebrew when you can't even carry a tune in English."
—**Elise, age 11**

66The hardest part? It's definitely getting your cheeks pinched by all those close-and-personal relatives.99 —Elliot, age 9

66Once you get Bar Mitzvahed, you might get called at five o'clock in the morning to make a minyan...Growing up has its downside.99 —Lou, age 12

66Not laughing and being embarrassed while the rabbi is pretty much describing your life like you were an angel or something.99 —Beth B., age 10

66Trying to remember all of your relatives' names, while you are saying: 'Wow, thank you so much, Aunt Whatsyourname?'99 —Jack T., age 11

66Since it's a big event, the hardest thing might be not having the excitement to look forward to once it's over.99 —Carey, age 10

66I think I might have trouble remembering when to bow...But I don't think God is too picky about that anyway.99 —Dustin, age 8

What Are Some Things That a Jewish Person Can Do That You Would Consider a Good Deed?

"Praying with your heart all opened up like a book."
—Susan, age 11

"Donating food to the homeless—whether they are Jewish or not."
—Toni, age 10

"Helping an elderly person to walk easy."
—Brittany, age 12

"Even little things count, like picking up someone's mail or newspaper when they are away...That's a good deed too."
—Carey, age 10

"Helping someone in a wheelchair to get somewhere real speedy."
—Jakob, age 5

"Lifting anybody up who needs a lift."
—Ezekial, age 4

“Do mitzvot...And do you know what? Mitzvot aren't just for kids; they're for grown-ups too.” —**Andy C., age 8**

“Just being a nurse or a teacher is like being an instrument of God.” —**Alana, age 9**

“Don't just give money to people who need it; give them your time and love.” —**Stan B., age 8**

“Do *tzedakah* and give away things you don't need anymore to poor people.” —**Aliya, age 6**

Rachel, age 11

"Planting a tree and trying to make the world more like the Garden of Eden was, before the apple thing happened and people got less perfect."

—Scott P., age 9

"Reach into your heart and see what's there...Being honest with yourself is a good deed in the eyes of God." —Aviva, age 12

"Being a good example for smaller kids...They might not know what a good deed is, and you could be the first one to show them." —Raphael, age 8

"Keeping kosher as a way to honor Jewish tradition, not just because you feel you have to do it." —Alexis, age 12

"Bake a cake and bring it over to your neighbor who is eighty and doesn't have any family nearby." —Lisa C., age 11

"Any Jewish person, or any person at all who helps me with my science homework—now that's a good deed by my standards." —Rich, age 11

Shira, age 11

What Responsibilities Does a Jewish Person Have in Relation to Other Jews and Judaism?

❝To be thankful and proud of being Jewish but not eat too many latkes, so you don't get to be too fat.❞   **—Mike, age 7**

❝You should kiss the Torah good morning when you see it.❞
—Rivka, age 7

❝Go to synagogue every Saturday morning...Cartoons are not a good excuse for not going.❞   **—David, age 8**

❝You should respect differences...Like you shouldn't tease somebody for wearing a yarmulke all the time. Did you ever think it might prevent hair loss?❞   **—Arnold, age 10**

❝Be Jewish with your whole heart and during your whole week...not just on Shabbat.❞   **—Rona, age 10**

❝We should keep Judaism up-to-date but also make sure it is the same religion that Abraham and his son started.❞
—Aaron P., age 10

“Following the laws of the Bible is big, but stuff that isn't written down, like not scaring kids that are smaller than you, is big too.” —**Jeremy, age 10**

“My Dad says you have a duty to have fun on Simchat Torah, so I try to do that the whole year-'round too.” —**Efraim, age 8**

“It's good for a person to remember their heritage... Especially when it's one that teaches you so much about how to be a good person.” —**Elaine, age 10**

“We have a responsibility to be responsible to other people.” —**Carey, age 10**

“Never forget that you are Jewish...Write yourself a note on your hand if you need to.” —**Isaiah, age 7**

Miles, age 7

What Responsibilities Does a Jewish Person Have in Relation to the World at Large?

“To see that God loves all kinds of people...Not just one color or religion.”
—Amy G., age 7

“Realize that getting hurt by someone is not a reason to try to hurt them back.”
—Carey, age 10

“Try to tell the world about God without shouting too loud in somebody else's ear.”
—Chaim, age 9

“Whenever you see something wrong in the world, try to change it and pray to God for strength.”
—Scott, age 9

“Never be silent against meanness...It could spread if you keep quiet.”
—Jamie, age 11

“Try to bring a little joy and happiness into the world every chance you get.”
—Robert, age 10

"Teach the world what Judaism is about: that God is the one and only God, and we are all connected to Him." —Edgar, age 12

"Be friendly to all kinds of people... Even girls." —Perchok, age 8

"Our biggest responsibility is to God. God made us so we should make the world the way He would want it...with a whole lot of love inside of it." —Janet D., age 9

Is It Hard Being Jewish?

"Only when you have to get up early for Hebrew school or when you have to fast on Yom Kippur...The rest is pretty easy."
—Frieda, age 9

"It's never hard if you believe in God and you know that God loves you."
—Bonnie, age 8

"It's easy to be Jewish so long as you start out in Jewish nursery school."
—Aliya, age 6

"Sometimes it's hard to be one of the only Jews in your school or neighborhood."
—Carey, age 10

"Standing up for prayers for an hour is hard...I wish I could talk to God about changing that."
—Ryan, age 11

"Celebrating holidays like Passover is more fun than it is difficult...Although, if I had to cook for thirty guests, I might feel different."
—Tamara, age 12

"Fifty years ago, it was the hardest thing in the world to be Jewish...We should appreciate how easy it is for us if you compare the two."
—**Donna, age 11**

"To be close to God is both hard and easy...It's hard because we can't see God but it's easy because God is with us even on the playground."
—**Solomon, age 8**

"It's easy to be Jewish...You just need a house, a *mezuzzah*, and a wall. Then you're all set."
—**Ronnie, age 7**

"The hardest thing is remembering all the blessings by heart. I always get the bread one wrong...I guess I should be a doctor instead of a cantor."
—**Nahum, age 8**

"Hard or easy, I like being Jewish. I think it builds character. I wouldn't trade it in."
—**Marty K., age 11**

How Is the Jewish Religion Similar or Different from Other Religions?

"We eat more matzah but we pray just the same."
—**Keith, age 8**

"We were the first ones to talk to God but now we share God with anybody else who asks about Him." —**Robert, age 10**

"Jewish people have different rules, like no milk and meat together, but I think the values about love and honesty are just the same."
—**Toni, age 10**

"We think that the Messiah hasn't come yet, but some people think he was already here...Me personally, I'm pretty sure it will be a girl, because it's going to take a woman's touch to heal the world."
—**Aviva, age 12**

"Jewish people have some different last names, like Levine is one. But names aren't important; what matters is being true to your beliefs."
—**Mindy, age 9**

“All the religions have this in common: We all have people in them that are loved by God.**”**
—Johanna, age 7

“Temple might be something like church, except they have more pancake breakfasts and we have more bagels and lox ones.**”**
—David P., age 8

“Judaism is different in that Jews usually eat kosher foods, but it's similar to other religions because Judaism teaches you to care about others.**”**
—Carey, age 10

“I think we're all in the same boat together...We've been there since Noah's Ark.**”**
—Wendy M., age 11

“Some of us have T-shirts that say 'Shalom' on them.**”**
—Norman, age 7

Jenna & Margaret, age 10

Thoughts on the Holocaust from the Third Generation After

"It's hard for me to talk about it...But I think it's even hard for grown-ups too."
—**Olivia, age 9**

"I always feel this dull throbbing feeling when I talk about it."
—**Mallory, age 11**

"I know that there was a war and terrible things happened... That because you were Jewish, or just because of something else, like you had funny-colored hair, you would be treated like you weren't a human being."
—**Brittany, age 12**

"It scares me. It happened to Jews. It could happen to me. It could happen again."
—**Janet D., age 9**

"I think about all the people having to leave their homes, and I think about Grandpa who was in the Holocaust and I think about Great-Grandma, and it makes me feel sad."
—**Carey, age 10**

"I don't think there are many words to describe the Holocaust...Rage might be one of them." —Esther, age 11

"I went to the Holocaust Museum in Washington. I heard about a boy my age who got separated from his parents and never saw them again...I realize that could have been me." —Arnold, age 10

"Helpless...The Holocaust leaves me feeling helpless...I wish there was something I could do." —Anita, age 10

"I don't think there was ever more evil in the world than there was at that time." —Ellen, age 10

"Kids like me shouldn't forget that it happened...It's up to us to tell people when we grow up." —Rena, age 9

"The Holocaust is one topic you don't really want to talk about, but once you start, it's hard to stop...I guess that's because people are still trying to make sense of it." —Rachel Y., age 11

What Does Israel Represent to You?

"It's like one big Jewish reunion." —**Carey, age 10**

"It's a nation in the Middle East that has the most Bibles and the most shofars in the world." —**Jakob, age 5**

"Maybe there used to be slaves working in that part of the world, but Israel shows that freedom can be there too." —**Aliya, age 6**

"When we go to services we ask God to say hello to Israel and watch over it real good." —**Ezekial, age 4**

"I think of the people in Israel as cousins...but real close cousins." —**Arnold, age 10**

"Israel is about deserts, tents, and stone houses, and it's all about God too." —**Lenore, age 9**

"Israel is like a candle that will never burn out." —**Ruth, age 10**

"It's a country where Jews from all over the world can come and feel at home...Even Jews from Antarctica can go there."

—Reuben, age 9

Shayna, age 7

A Brief Sample of Jewish Humor

"What did the matzah say to the farfel?...You know, farfel, you really break me up."

—**Mitchell, age 11**

"Why does the Jewish letter for 'A' *(alef)* look like a flower?...Because a 'B' always comes right after it."

—**Carey, age 10**

"I heard that Bible is just a French word for Torah. Is that true?"

—**Simon, age 4**

"Murray was Moses' agent. One day Murray said to Moses: 'Moses, ol' boy, I have a great new assignment for you, right from God. All you have to do is split the Red Sea.'

Moses was all upset, and he said back to Murray: 'Are you kidding? How am I going to do that? Dividing up the sea is going to be impossible!'

So Murray answered him: 'Not to worry. Would God leave you alone with this? No sir, no way. He promised me He's going to give you a staff to work with.'"

—**Jake, age 11**

"Why are all Jewish people good at packing? The answer is: If you had to move around in the desert for forty years, you would learn to travel light too.**"**

—Mark, age 12

Laura, age 10

"My grandmother...She's very generous, but most of all she's just a wonderful person."
—**Brittany, age 12**

"Was Noah Jewish? If he was, then I would pick him because he must have been real good at being a captain."
—**Samuel, age 8**

"The people who founded Israel...They had a lot of courage and plus it's not easy to grow fruit and plant so many trees right in the middle of the sand."
—**Chaim, age 9**

"Yitzhak Rabin...I admire him because he gave his life for peace."
—**Mordecai, age 12**

"Moses is the greatest Jewish hero because he allowed himself to go from a free man to a slave in order to save his people."
—**Evan, age 11**

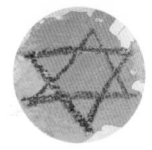

"Anybody who can read the Torah by heart is a hero...
It's really hard to read stuff without vowels." **—Mark, age 12**

"Joseph was a hero because he never lost his faith in God...
which is pretty hard when you are a lifer in Pharaoh's dungeon." **—Sholom, age 9**

"Have there ever been any Jewish quarterbacks? If not,
then I would say that King David was pretty good too." **—Ian, age 9**

"My Dad is my hero...Because he loves me and he watches
out for me." **—Carey, age 10**

"I think my Mother is a lady hero because she likes to pray...
God respects that." **—Janet D., age 9**

"Samson...He wasn't too big or almighty to ask God to forgive his sins, and so his strength came back to him."

—Steve, age 11

"My rabbi...He has so much love in him that he's taught all of us the real meaning of being a hero."

—Gary, age 12

"The Jewish person with the most money is not a hero; the one with the most good deeds and friends is."

—Jason D., age 11

"It could be Hillel or Maimonides or just my older brother... Actually, it's kind of a toss-up for me."

—Gordon, age 10

"Every person is a hero if they follow their own religion and they are true to themselves."

—Joshua, age 10

How Do You Think Being Jewish Will Change by the Time That You Grow Up?

❝All Jewish homes might have stained glass windows made in Israel...Even in the kitchens.❞ —**Carey, age 10**

❝Being Jewish might become real popular...They might even sell challahs at baseball games like they sell pretzels now.❞ —**Eli, age 8**

❝People will get Bar Mitzvahed three and four times...when you are twenty-three and thirty-three, not just thirteen...That way you can't forget what you've learned about being Jewish.❞ —**Moshe, age 8**

❝There might be more Jewish people in the world, since I'll be a mother by then and I plan on having ten children.❞ —**Mandy, age 7**

❝Yarmulkes might change colors just by pushing a button on them.❞ —**Jody, age 8**

"There might be a *tallit* for ladies that has pink and purple stripes on it."
—**Rona, age 10**

"There will be a Jewish network on TV and it will have a menorah for a symbol, instead of like they have a peacock now."
—**Sheldon, age 11**

"There will be a Jewish President by then... and I bet it will be a girl."
—**Dina, age 8**

"There will be computer programs with the Torah on them."
—**Reuben, age 9**

"Kosher hot dogs will replace pizza as the number one food in America."
—**Scott, age 9**

"We'll be able to travel to Israel in fifteen minutes. They'll have Jerusalem specials, where you go for a Jewish dinner and then come back to your synagogue for dessert in the same day."
—**Rena, age 8**

"Maybe peace will be
even more of a real thing
than it is now?"
—Sheila H., age 9

Miriam, age 7

Reflections on Being Jewish

"I like being Jewish because *dreidels* are the world's best tops." **—Stephen J., age 8**

"Being Jewish is a good way to get to know God up close and personal...Since He seems to talk to us a lot." **—Stan, age 10**

"When you're Jewish, the whole world looks like your grandma to you...Kind of warm and smiling and friendly." **—Jenny, age 11**

"Being Jewish means eating hot knishes in the wintertime." **—Shana, age 9**

"Being Jewish is cool because it gives you an extra language to speak." **—Evan, age 11**

"Being Jewish might change a little on the outside over the years, but it will always have a lot to do with celebrating the life that God gives to us." **—Mordecai, age 12**

"If you're Jewish, everybody in the world is kind of related to you."   —David, age 8

"A Jewish religious person is someone who loves God totally, and loves all the people just like God does." —Rachel Y., age 11

"The religion teaches that it's the kind of person you are that matters most of all."   —Toni, age 10

"Being Jewish just makes me feel all good inside."   —Carey, age 10

"I think Jewish people are so friendly because they know what it feels like to be left out, like because of prejudice."   —Daniel J., age 9

—Paul, age 7

"I'm Proud to Be

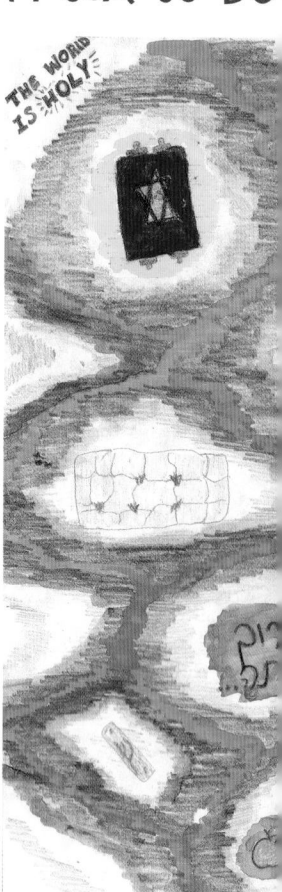

❝We gave the world Moses and bagels, and the world has been real holy ever since.**❞**
                                        —Mitchell, age 11

❝It gives me a chance to celebrate Shabbat.**❞**
                                        —Aliya, age 6

❝Jewish is just the way I was born and I'm just glad about it.**❞**   —Carey, age 10

❝Jewish people have given so much to mankind...Look at Einstein and Elie Wiesel, just to name a couple.**❞**   —Mark, age 12

❝We are a peace-loving people.**❞**
                                        —Scott, age 9

❝I love to eat matzah brei.**❞**
                                        —Jessie, age 5

Jewish Because..."

"I'm proud to be Jewish because my rabbi looks like Abraham!" 　　　　　　**—Mitchell, age 11**

"Kindness and charity are our way of life." 　　　　　　**—Evan, age 11**

"Because we have never given up even when the chips were down, and that's why we still exist today—even though we are small in number...And, oh yeah, God had a lot to do with it too." 　　　　　　**—Anita, age 10**

"I'm proud to know that Torahs are more valuable than gold." 　　　　　　**—Sheldon, age 11**

"I'm proud to be Jewish because we have taught the world a lot about God." 　　　　　　**—Sandra, age 10**

Rachel, age 11

The Artists

Amy Abramowitz, North Carolina: *Shofar*

Kate Arian, New Jersey: *Noah's Ark*

Adina Berger, New Jersey: *Chicken Soup*

Sofia Corporan, Washington, D.C.: *Reciting Prayers*

Cara Davies, Ontario: *Rainbow Star of David*

Sarah Dobkin, Illinois: *Miriam in Her Tent*

Igor Dobrusin, Massachusetts: *Mezuzzah*

Miles Fineburg, Pennsylvania: *Alef*

Noah Gereboff, Arizona: *Celebrating Shabbat*

Goldie Leah Gibbs, Wisconsin: *Miriam and the Baby Moses*

Shira Gordon, Illinois: *Dancing with the Torah; Planting a Tree*

Maddie Greil, New York: *Star of David*

Sydney Howells, Pennsylvania: *Pharaoh's Chariot*

Laura Krassner, New York: *The World is Holy* (Globe)

Lauren Kutner, Pennsylvania: *Hula Bagel; Bagel Tambourine; Bagel Toss; Bagel Binoculars; Bagel Bracelet; Bagel Boarding*

Ilana Lerman, Wisconsin: *Menorah*

Avital Levavi, New Jersey: *Tower of Babel* (pink)

Valerie Levin, New Jersey: *Blue and White Balloon*

Michael London, New Jersey: *Tower of Babel* (blue)

Paul Mattos, North Carolina: *The Dreidels*

Jenna Rosen and Margaret Kurtzman New York: *T-shirt with Shalom*

Adina Rubin, Illinois: *Drinking Grape Juice*

Judah Rubin, Illinois: *Moses and the Burning Bush*

Shayna Schwartzman, Illinois: *Star of David*

Lauren Steinberg, New York: *Jewish Candle*

Arielle Tonkin, New York: *Shabbat Wine*

Rachel Vale, Ontario: *The World is Holy*

Alina Zaltzman, Ontario: *Seder Plate*

Miriam Zander, New Jersey: *Noah and the Dove*